SELF DISCIPLINE

An Essential Guide For Men To Improve Self-Discipline And Focus, Build Good Habits To Achieve Your Goals (Stop Procrastinating and Start Living 2022)

Dana Green

INTRODUCTION

People with higher degrees of self-control spend less time debating whether to indulge in harmful behaviors and can make more positive choices with more ease. They do not make choices based on their emotions or inclinations. Instead, they make wise choices. As a consequence, people are generally happy in their lives. Rules, regulations, and punishment are not examples of discipline.

It is not about compliance, obedience, or enforcing rules. It is not rigid, monotonous, or always doing the same thing.

Discipline is not something that you are forced to do. It is the process of learning and using purposeful criteria in order to achieve meaningful objectives.

We may have a feeling of what it does for us and why we want it since it is a choice and we are learning how to obtain more and greater discipline. We're trying to figure out how to get more and better alternatives. There are more and better options.

When you perceive discipline as a choice, you are in command, not anybody or anything else. More discipline, more alternatives, and more control. There is less discipline, diversity, and control. Isn't that right?

When we lose our discipline and capacity to choose, we give up control to other people, external circumstances, and the inherent unpredictability of life. We wander and end up as a pawn in the hands of circumstances.

Table of Content

CHAPTER 1

THE SCIENCE AND PSYCHOLOGY OF SELF-DISCIPLINE

Self-discipline is typically an act of will; therefore, understanding how the human mind works are critical. This is done in order to translate comprehension into a higher feeling of self-control. Over millions of years, the human brain has become even more sophisticated.

Psychology, as a human activity, has cast some light on the mysteries of the mind, eventually enabling us to observe how things impact or motivate individuals and how our environment affects how we respond to things that happen.

Self-Image

A man's perception of himself influences how he behaves in the environment.

This is influenced by how he was reared or the individuals who have surrounded him.

The environment in which he grew up influenced how he perceives himself. Some men have poor self-esteem, leading them to think that they are undeserving of excellent things or that they are incapable of reaching perfection.

Others, on the other hand, have an exaggerated sense of self-worth and feel that they deserve everything without having to accomplish anything. These individuals, however formidable on appearance, are empty on the inside.

Cracks in their impenetrable exterior will reveal a tremendous vulnerability that they have spent a lifetime concealing. If a guy wants to be a real alpha male, he must know the truth about himself and not succumb to insecurity or the urge to take the easy way out by hiding behind a mask.

However, there is no assurance that we will be able to comprehend ourselves gone; in fact, even psychology has failed to offer us a conclusive answer solution.

However, if you want to be an alpha man, you must be receptive to critique. Negative feedback allows the guy to deviate from his current course and better himself. However, focusing on negative criticism will not help.

Negative feedback is only useful for determining if we are on the correct track. You must, however, determine if the feedback originates from trustworthy and credible sources.

People often lie about what they think of you for political reasons. As a result, you should only take input from those you know to be brutally honest, such as a mentor or even adversaries. Enemies have no interest in you and, by definition, despise you. As a result, they will have no desire to sugarcoat anything. They will be completely and utterly honest.

It is best not to get very emotional about what people say; instead, use it to develop and attain—not for them, but for yourself—the ideal you want to achieve or the cause you are fighting for.

Control Point

A guy on the road to self-improvement must choose whether he blames others or himself for his circumstances. If the guy constantly blames others for everything that occurs to him, it is stated that his locus of control is external, which indicates that he surrenders his authority to fate or "destiny." This is the mentality of a weak guy, especially if he believes he has no influence over what happens to him. He is weak-minded and weak-willed, and he believes that everything that occurs to him is the result of random circumstances or other people—this is a lazy and weak attitude to life.

A guy with an internal locus of control, on the other hand, tends to regard everything as his fault, and if this goes too far, he becomes too overwhelmed by what is happening to him and even to the world.

He may blame himself for something that occurred to someone unconnected to him, which is implausible. Returning to the subject of self-image, the alpha male must have accurate knowledge about himself in order to act on it.

The alpha male must be balanced and have a locus of control, which implies he must take responsibility for his actions. Taking on greater responsibility enhances his capacity to take bigger chances and enables him to venture outside of his comfort zone.

Conditioning, Classical

To refute the notion that psychology was an armchair pseudoscience, the behaviourist movement, led by psychologist Ivan Pavlov, introduced the scientific method into the discipline through experiments. Pavlov was able to demonstrate the process of training and conditioning by measuring how much dogs salivate when a bell indicates food is rung. The experimenter removes the food after ringing the bell. Soon, even when he does not bring out food, the sheer ringing of the bell has been demonstrated to cause the dogs to behave as if they are getting ready for food. Conditioning is another method to apply this notion, as is reward and punishment.

People and animals prefer to avoid punishment and instead seek out benefits. As a result, incentives motivate us to continue doing what we were doing in order to reap the pleasure of the reward.

Punishments function in the other direction. Thus a balance of both reward and punishment will successfully train a person to do a certain behavior. We were born with the ability to control ourselves, and we may deliberately employ it to accomplish the kind of activity we want to learn.

Consider how much suffering you will endure if you do not act. For example, how much discomfort would you experience if you did not prepare for your exam? Perhaps you will not be able to graduate. Consider the short-term agony of studying against the long-term agony of failing to graduate. Consider the reward or pleasure you will get if you complete the research. You will get a diploma and be appreciated by others. In this manner, you may fool yourself into doing things you don't want to do.

Motivational Psychology

When asked who would win in an arena between a lion and a man, most people say the lion since it is more powerful and has evolved to be stronger than the man. Unless the guy is the legendary Hercules, the lion will undoubtedly eat him.

This, however, does not account for the millions of years of evolution that humanity has undergone. Humans have developed a more complicated intellect as well as the capacity to invent and construct weapons. So, a lion vs a man equipped with weapons would be a more even fight?

Humans are more complicated than animals, as shown by our drive to become more important than ourselves. This book is already proof of that. Thus, in order to motivate a guy to become greater than himself, he must first understand what he is fighting for. He needs a goal as well as a means of determining whether or not he has met it.

Even the most seasoned fighter will fail if he does not know why he is fighting. A guy on a mission is unstoppable.

Once a guy has decided on his aim, he must take action.

Success is being and doing what you want right now, and that can only be accomplished if you move quickly and as if success is already here. The objective will be accomplished soon, even if you don't think about it. It is also necessary to have faith in the process or habit by exercising self-control on a regular basis.

CHAPTER 2

HOW SELF-DISCIPLINE CAN IMPROVE YOUR HAPPINESS

If you lack self-discipline, your business's success is compromised.

You may create business objectives, but don't you procrastinate and lose focus if no one keeps you accountable?

This is something that many company owners do. We often depend so heavily on the counsel of others that we fail to regulate ourselves effectively. Then we start rationalizing, assuring ourselves that it is not our fault that we did not do our job.

After all, we were missing the person who normally leads our activities. Therefore, we were doomed to fail.

This style of thinking encourages the destructive practice of seeking excuses to fail. Our failures build-up, our self-esteem and self-love crumble, and we add to the stress in our lives.

This is terrible since self-control can be learned. The human brain is a complex computer that may be programmed with devotion and self-control.

You might make an attempt to become more disciplined and acquire control over your life. Self-control is crucial for everyone, particularly in today's world when everyone is wired and addicted 24 hours a day, seven days a week. Distractions abound, providing you with lots of excuses to avoid doing what you need to do to achieve your objectives.

Let's take a look at the advantages of conscious living to give you the motivation to work hard on becoming motivated, focused, and self-disciplined entrepreneur.

Self-discipline will be necessary at some time, whether you want to be more successful in business or just get more of the personal pleasures you seek. Life isn't always easy, but self-control can lead to deliberate, conscious action that transforms a difficult period into rich rewards and self-esteem.

It's a huge relief to discover you're the boss. You are not alone if you always feel as though you are at the mercy of others. Most individuals have the impression that they have little control over their life. The more often you can take charge of your life and ignore outside influences that try to dominate or distract you, the better.

There is only one person on this planet who has influence over your actions while also having your best interests at heart... and that is you.

The more self-discipline you cultivate, the more you take charge of your life rather than allowing others to guide it.

Here are five ways that self-control might help you be happier:

1. Self-Control Increases Self-Esteem and Self-Love

When you feel good about yourself, your life improves organically.

This is due to the fact that self-esteem and self-love are contingent on you living a life that reflects your beliefs. This will need self-control.

By default, the world will not provide you with a goal-achieving and value-fulfilling destiny. Work is sometimes necessary, and this requires self-discipline.

Take a look at the definition of self-discipline. It entails doing what has to be done, even if it is unpleasant. When you endure in the face of adversity and keep a laser-like concentration, you will find yourself more regularly accomplishing objectives and key milestones.

How did you feel the last time you had to work hard to acquire something you wanted? Wasn't that a wonderful sensation? Intentional self-discipline helps you feel good about yourself through building self-esteem and self-belief, which leads to future rewards and successes.

2. Your path to success becomes easier and more rewarding.

This advantage is substantial unless you get a big inheritance from a long-lost relative and do not need to work for a livelihood. You've seen how confidence increases your chances of success in any effort.

The notion of success spawning success is well-known in the business.

This implies that when you achieve more accomplishments and objectives, obtaining future ones gets simpler and easier.

3. You Consciously Improve

Your brain keeps track of how much you achieve as your self-discipline improves. Every day, you are presented with a plethora of alternatives and decisions. When feasible, your brain attempts to automate those decision-making processes.

You had to remember to feed your pet every day, change its water, play with it, and clean up after it when you were a youngster. After a time, this becomes an unconscious habit. You most likely caught yourself feeding your pet without even realizing it.

When you initially attempted to ride a bicycle, you fell a lot. You had scrapes and bruises, and you probably cried as well. It takes a lot of self-discipline at that early age to get back on the bike. You ultimately perfected the art of bicycle riding to the point that you no longer question your ability to do so.

Self-discipline helps you perform better in a range of situations.

As your skill develops, the time it takes you to perform a job decreases, giving you more time to do what you like. The gifted but slow athlete will ultimately give way to the industrious, self-disciplined competitor with less natural skill.

This is due to the fact that self-control makes you more successful and competent.

4. Your Personal Relationships Will Improve

It is impossible to keep commitments to others if you are unable to keep them to yourself. This implies that if you want to develop deeper, more meaningful relationships with the people that are important to you, you may.

All you need to do is work on your self-control. You may readily anticipate how you will treat others by seeing how you treat yourself.

Others respect someone who has self-control and self-discipline. This means that you attract others who, like you, want to increase their abilities to govern their own life. Your reliability shows through, and your connections grow stronger as a result.

Self-discipline also helps to strengthen your relationships in another manner. It gives you the courage to let go of those who are keeping you from living a full and meaningful life.

5. Identify Your True Priorities and Values Begin to Appear

There are several instances of successful entrepreneurs who sought riches at the expense of all else in their life. Many of these stories include a change of heart. The person who emphasized money above everything else recognized that this was not in his or her best interests, and self-control got them back on track.

When you adopt a stern approach to self-government and self-direction, you begin to compare all of your actions. You learn to think before you act, which shows what is really important to you.

Self-discipline is a fantastic method for determining what is genuinely important in your life.

What you believe you greatly value may not necessarily be what you naturally and earnestly want deep down within.

What Is the Importance of Self-Discipline in Success?

Self-discipline is the key to success in life. You won't be able to achieve in life until you have it. Successful individuals would constantly tell you to keep your discipline. But the question remains, "Why is self-discipline so important in life?"

Self-control allows you to become an unstoppable force of energy in your life, helping you to reach your maximum potential.

If you want to be successful in life, the first thing you must do is discipline yourself.

Reasons Why Self-Discipline Is Required for Success

1. Self-discipline becomes a habit.

Habits have the power to either make or break you. Self-discipline develops a habit in your life that can only be obtained via discipline.

Because most individuals are lethargic, they never maintain a sense of discipline in their lives. On the other hand, laziness is a habit.

People that are successful train themselves to work and maintain consistency in their efforts. And it rapidly gets ingrained. This is what makes them successful in life.

2. It assists with work completion.

Self-discipline is essential to complete tasks. It might be anything, such as agreeing to read a certain number of books or finishing tasks within a certain time range.

When you push yourself to accomplish everything, you construct a personality that revolves around it.

This exercise raises you to the level of achiever in your life.

Success requires self-discipline. Because it enables you to be consistent in your life, and consistency enables you to accomplish everything you want in life.

3. It improves focus.

We live in a world full of distractions. Self-discipline helps you to focus on your objectives. It helps you stay focused on the tasks you need to perform in order to succeed.

When you are focused on your objective, you will complete all of your tasks.

People who are successful have razor-sharp concentration.

They are always looking forward to achieving their life's objectives and triumphs.

This allows individuals to achieve huge success in their lives.

4. It boosts self-esteem and work ethic.

Those that believe in themselves and work the hardest in the room will be successful. Self-discipline assists you to improve your work ethic while also increasing your self-esteem.

You improve your work ethic by adhering to your discipline.

It will help you achieve your objectives.

Completing your aims on a daily basis, on the other hand, will begin to boost your self-esteem and confidence in your job.

This is why self-discipline is so important.

5. It helps you achieve mastery.

Those who are masters rather than novices are successful. You must be a master at something if you want to be successful.

You become a master by putting in the time and committing up to 10,000 hours to a single assignment.

Mastery requires discipline. The majority of individuals fail because they lack mastery over any skill. Successful individuals, on the other hand, concentrate on a single task and master it.

So, self-discipline leads to mastery, and mastery leads to success.

6. It helps you become the best version of yourself.

Success will come only when you earn it. You will not be able to attain success with your existing personality. As a consequence, you must strive for advancement on a regular basis.

To be the finest version of yourself in life, you must try to be the best version of yourself.

Self-discipline helps you to improve yourself on a daily basis. When you do anything on a consistent basis, you grow better and better every day.

As a consequence, self-discipline is critical for personal success and advancement.

Self-discipline is the most important part of success. If you want to be successful in life, you must be disciplined. Otherwise, disciplined individuals will knock you out.

You have an infinite capacity to accomplish your best degree of success in life. All you need is a little self-control.

So, rather than wasting time, go out there and start doing things that will get you closer to your life objectives.

CHAPTER 3

THE ALPHA MALE DISCIPLINE

Self-discipline is essential for personal and professional development. It is the driving force behind attention, focus, and achieving one's purpose, goals, and objectives. One of the most crucial characteristics of alpha is mastery of self-discipline.

The persistent attention of alpha and his unyielding and adaptable temperament allow him to discipline himself and fulfil his life objectives. On the other hand, discipline is difficult to sustain in the absence of a feeling of duty and accountability.

On the other hand, discipline is a distinguishing feature of an alpha male. This attitude feeds his desire and ambition to achieve in whatever he does or to survive wherever he finds himself. There are various stages for those who want to nurture the habit of discipline and acquire this alpha characteristic.

These methods will boost a person's focus level, give them an edge, lead them closer to their passion, and help them accomplish whatever they seek in life.

Listed below are numerous methods for developing the habit of discipline.

Resist Your Cravings

Discipline requires exercising control over one's impulses and being able to resist every temptation to live and sustain an unhealthy lifestyle, such as smoking excessively, eating highly processed foods, or becoming preoccupied with social media. Unnecessary activities detract from a person's ability to accomplish what he wishes or aspires to achieve. To break away from this habit, an exercise or workout regimen and diet plan will assist a person in being more disciplined with his behaviours and choices. It is tough to participate in a monotonous activity, but motivating oneself to exercise will make it simpler to adhere to routines and develop the discipline to finish tasks once they are started.

Following a good food plan is one of the most crucial aspects of discipline since it offers the fuel and mental clarity needed to complete whatever a person has to do.

Set Achievable Objectives

Having a vision and clearly identifying the mission statement, short-term and long-term goals can assist a person in outlining some attainable goals and objectives.

As a result, when a person lacks insight and a sense of direction, they may simply return to their objectives to help them realign and attain the amount of discipline required to accomplish what they need to.

Be Consistent and Persistent

Maintaining discipline and attention requires being persistent and keeping to daily objectives, purposes, and goals. Never give up on your vision when confronted with failure, uncertainty, fear, or other distressing feelings that may be harmful to your aims and objectives. Discipline is loving the pain and persisting in reaching for goals that seem difficult and hard to attain. When you've mastered this, you'll be able to go outside of your comfort zone and investigate and tackle your fears and concerns. To build discipline, you must be able to experience pain and learn to welcome adversity when it arises.

Improve Your Organization

Discipline is being orderly, and studies have shown that a person's surroundings frequently reflects how their brain performs. Organising everything around you is one of the finest methods to develop discipline, whether at home, the job, a place of worship, a recreational area, or anywhere else.

Make a daily schedule and plan

Schedules and daily schedules will allow a person to stay on track with their activities, purpose, objectives, and interests regardless of what happens. A plan and a timetable assist a person in avoiding useless and unproductive activities while concentrating on one's own physical, emotional, and mental growth. According to studies, having a daily plan and timetable is one of the simplest methods to efficiently manage one's life.

Embrace Gratitude

To retain concentration, it is critical to continually look ahead to the future and avoid obsessing on previous errors or failures since they induce worry, fear, anxiety, and stress, all of which are detrimental to success. To establish discipline, it is best to practice thankfulness on a regular basis; this will help to balance the desire for achievement with a good outlook on the present. To succeed, no matter where you are or where you find yourself in life, being thankful for what you have today is the greatest approach to becoming disciplined.

Every day, meditate

Meditation aids in the relaxation of the mind, the relaxation of the nerves, and the relief of tension. It is advised that a person meditates for at least twenty minutes every day in order to develop self-discipline.

This may be done before or after work, at home, at school, or wherever is most convenient for you. Being able to meditate on a regular basis can help a person become more disciplined, quiet, and mentally aware of what is going on in his life. The health advantages of meditation are many and overwhelming, and the changes seen when a person begins meditating on a daily basis are useful and encouraging for anybody who aspires to be valuable.

Get Plenty of Sleep

Getting a good night's sleep is an important aspect of self-discipline. To improve your health, nourish your skin, and become less irritable, make it a habit to go to bed early and get up on time every day. Regardless of how you optimize your sleeping routine, research suggests that it is critical to receive at least eight hours of sleep each night. It will be beneficial to remove distractions and firmly adhere to a sleeping routine that allows you at least eight hours of sleep each night in order to achieve this discipline.

CHAPTER 4

THE POWER OF POSITIVE THINKING

Discipline issues may severely impact both your personal and professional life. It's time to stand up for yourself, do what you know you need to do to succeed, and take charge of your life.

This is something that positive thinking may help you with.

I used the words "positive thinking" rather than "mind over matter." The principle of positive thinking is that your thoughts influence your actions.

When you consider anything (any work) a challenge, it becomes more difficult to do. When you perceive anything (anything) to be tough, it becomes more difficult than it needs to be.

Positive Thinking's Power

And Why You Should Use It Every Day

Positive thinking is, well, positive thinking. It is the inverse of negative thinking. But, perhaps more crucially, it is the power to force oneself to think positively - about anything. As we all know, your attitude or conduct distinguishes successful individuals from failed ones.

Nothing can stop you from living your ideal life if you can think positively and have a good mindset. Nothing will demotivate or discourage you because you will continue to push on because that is what you believe in - yourself and your potential to achieve.

Your conduct is dictated by your ideas, which is why you must have a good mindset in order to live a successful life.

What Is the Process of Positive Thinking?

Because our conscious mind outnumbers our subconscious mind, you must be optimistic. The subconscious mind has power over all of the body's operations and takes into account everything that occurs in our lives — whether we want it or not. It goes through life assuming that we would fail at everything we do, which is why it never really trusts us.

This is why it is so simple for us to make mistakes - we are attempting to achieve something that our subconscious mind believes we are incapable of achieving. This is why, if we can control our ideas, we can control our actions, and hence the result.

One thing you must realize is that your ideas have greater power than your deeds. You will ultimately do something horrible if you think about it. If you think about doing something nice, there's a decent probability you'll do it. This is why you should focus on the positive aspects of your life and work to make them a reality.

If you feel the work is too tough for you, your mind will make it so. You'll get irritated and try for an easy way out. If you feel the work is doable, your mind will make it so, and even if it takes five times as long as it should, you will finally accomplish what you set out to do in the first place.

Again, this is due to our subconscious brains, which are continuously seeking our approval and want us to be in charge at all times. This is why it is critical for us to be optimistic in our thinking; if we are not, we make it much too easy for our subconscious mind to take over and make bad judgments - all in the name of proving that we are human and hence incapable of doing something as basic as being positive.

So, how do you cope with self-doubt? Positive thinking is the solution. You must train your mind to think positively about everything you want. For example, if you want to lose weight, you must be optimistic about everything you do. When you look at food, convince yourself that it tastes delicious and constantly remind yourself of how healthy you are becoming. If you find yourself being negative about anything in your life, employ positive thinking to modify your thoughts and, as a result, your behavior.

As easy as this may seem, the issue arises when we must begin doing something tough, like studying for an exam or beginning a new diet. Because we don't believe we can accomplish it, our minds want to quit up straight away. This is when the power of positive thinking comes into play once again. You will discover that by being optimistic and believing in yourself, you will be able to accomplish more in life than others who are usually negative.

How Do You Maintain Your Positive Attitude?

So, how can you maintain your optimistic attitude? It isn't simple, but it is doable if you set your mind to it. It will take time, but it will be worth it in the end. Here are a few suggestions to assist you to maintain your mind in a pleasant state:

If anything goes wrong, don't linger on it.

Consider what went wrong and why it happened that way - but don't dwell on it for too long. Make sure that whatever occurred did not stay in your brain, and consider how you may better yourself for the next time.

Believe in yourself if you want to accomplish anything.

Consider what it will take to reach your goals, and don't allow anything to stand in your way. If you want to lose weight, convince yourself that you will lose all of the weight you desire and keep saying it until it becomes a reality.

Surround yourself with positive individuals to keep yourself optimistic.

Surrounding yourself with negative people will only make it more difficult for you to remain cheerful. If you want to be happy, hang out with other individuals who are cheerful and optimistic.

Every day, keep a diary and put down your ideas. This will help you to express yourself and provide you with a place to discharge your ideas when they get too much for you. Make sure that everything you write is uplifting and encouraging since if it isn't, it will just add to your issues rather than solve them.

Do you need some assistance getting started? Here are some pointers to help you remain optimistic in any situation:

Make a list of what you desire.

Make your points clear. Write out precisely how you want to accomplish it, and be sure to include a description of any obstacles. Once you have this, read it every day to remind yourself of all of the actions you need to do to reach your goals.

Keep an eye on your ideas and make sure they are constantly good.

Take notice of when you begin to think negative ideas and replace them with positive ones. If a bad idea enters your head unexpectedly, attempt to suppress it by thinking about it in a different manner or by writing down all of the positive outcomes of thinking that way.

Maintain a positive mindset.

Don't be concerned if you don't obtain what you want; there will always be something better around the corner. If things aren't going well, try not to lose your cool and don't allow it to get to you.

Keep a cheerful attitude and concentrate on the wonderful things in life.

Be truthful to yourself.

If you don't identify your issue areas, you'll never be able to alter them. Examine your life and determine where you need to improve. Consider what actions you can take to make these improvements a reality.

You will never acquire what you desire if you do not do this.

Be assured. Many people will question you and attempt to dissuade you from pursuing your goals, but don't listen to them. Confidence is essential for making your aspirations a reality. If a difficulty develops, trust that everything will work out for the best - because it always does!

Thank you on a daily basis. Be thankful for anything nice that comes your way. Admit it: things would be a lot worse if you didn't have your friends, family, and opportunities.

Never give up on your ambitions. You may not get everything you want in life, but never lose faith in yourself or what is possible.

CHAPTER 5

WORK UNTIL YOU FINALLY ACQUIRE YOUR CHANGE OF IDENTITY

So far, this book has given you all of the skills, insights, and guidance you need to start living the life of a real alpha guy. However, before the whole picture can be realised, one more piece of the jigsaw must be set in position. Setting objectives is an important part of this process.

The significance of establishing objectives cannot be emphasised.

While many individuals assume that their inability to make their dreams a reality is due to a lack of finances, time, or energy, the plain fact is that most people fall short owing to a lack of objectives.

Goals transform fantasies into doable tasks because actions may be made daily to get to the desired destination. Goals, in short, are what transform abstract and intangible aspirations into measurable realities.

To alter your life in any manner, shape, or form, you must first establish the required objectives.

What Is a Goal, Exactly?

Many individuals erroneously connect objectives with dreams. As a result, if you desire to be wealthy, you may state that your objective is to be wealthy.

Regrettably, this isn't correct. It is more accurate to state that your dream is to be wealthy. The aim is the step or series of stages in the strategy that will take you to your dream. Recognizing your goal is just the first step; knowing your dream is the next.

The next stage is to figure out how you're going to get there. You should probably plan your route. Depending on how far you have to travel, you may have to stop once or twice. Planning the route include determining how long it will take, which roads to take, and whether or not to stop along the way.

This is the act of establishing objectives. Each road you take is a goal, and each halt is a goal; every aspect of the trip is a goal, even when you leave and return. They are quantifiable acts that will take you closer to your goal.

This is where the majority of individuals fall short. They never take the time to create a route to go to where they want to go because they confuse the dream for a goal. They almost never take the initial step because they are unclear which one to take. When you map your route, you know where to go and when to go, enabling you to take the activities required to successfully realise your ambition.

Methods for Setting Effective Goals

Setting objectives isn't always enough in life, just as it isn't always enough in everything else. Instead, you must establish the appropriate objectives in the appropriate manner. When it comes to attaining your objectives, this will make all the difference.

Fortunately, there is a simple formula for defining realistic goals called the "SMARTER" goal system, and it works as follows:

Make careful to establish explicit objectives at all times. Instead of stating you want to lose weight, establish a goal of achieving a specific weight, such as 180 pounds. This is a particular objective that will allow you to quickly measure your progress.

Quantifiable

The next stage is to establish a measurable aim. In order to attain a goal weight, you must first determine where you are now. Thus, if you weigh 200 pounds, your quantifiable target is to shed 20 pounds.

Actionable

This is when you start plotting your strategy for reaching your overarching objective. If you want to drop twenty pounds, you might establish goals like eating better meals or exercising on a regular basis. This transforms the aim from an aspiration to a doable action.

Realistic

People often make the error of establishing objectives that are too lofty to attain. If you want to lose twenty pounds, you may divide the objective into four smaller goals of dropping five pounds every week. This alleviates the stress of an "all or nothing" situation, making it simpler to achieve your goals.

Time-Bound

There are two components to this aspect of goal planning. The first factor is when you begin. Decide when you will begin acting if you wish to reduce weight. The deadline is the following component. This is the point at which you hope to attain your aim. As a result, your new aim should be to drop five pounds in one week, beginning tomorrow.

Evaluate

You may begin analysing your progress if you have a measurable target and a timetable.

If you have only lost one pound halfway through your seven-day deadline, you can consider increasing your efforts—perhaps by exercising more, eating better, or extending the deadline. In the end, changing the goal is always preferable to abandoning it entirely.

Reward

The final stage of goal setting is to reward yourself for your accomplishments. For example, if you lose five pounds, you can choose to reward yourself by purchasing a DVD you've been eyeing or another relatively inexpensive item that serves as an incentive. This will not only motivate you to keep going but will also train your mind to seek to reach the objectives you set. When you reach the major objective, you may treat yourself to new clothing that will show off your new appearance as a reward.

Setting SMARTER objectives boosts your chances of success, which will alter your life in a number of major ways.

First and foremost, your self-confidence will become stronger with each objective you accomplish. As a result, as you accomplish more objectives, your confidence will rise, giving you the courage to pursue bigger and more ambitious ambitions. The second way this will affect your life is that it will boost your overall success. Each objective will make your life better in some manner. As a result, as you achieve more objectives, you will be ready to set even more, which will enhance your life immensely and allow you to live the life of your dreams.

Specific Objectives for the Alpha Male

Now that you understand the significance of goals and how to establish them. The third phase is to establish precise objectives for an alpha guy. The following are some objectives that can assist you in developing the alpha male lifestyle that you seek and deserve:

Improve Your Image: This might include your clothing, your body, and even your grooming practices. As a result, you must divide this overarching aim into smaller, more attainable objectives. The first thing you should do is enhance your haircut. Allow yourself thirty days to discover a stylist who can assist you in achieving the ideal style for you. Then you'll want to focus on bringing your weight back to where it should be.

Allow oneself thirty days to lose weight (if that is a goal that can be accomplished in that period). Finally, you'll want to revamp your clothes. Allow yourself another thirty days to modify your wardrobe style and get the alpha masculine appearance that will draw all the proper attention. Make this your last stage since you'll need to be at your ideal weight and have a hairdo in place to determine which garments work best for you.

Enhance Your Self-Image: This is another aim with multiple facets. Establishing your values is one component. Spend a week or two reflecting on the things that genuinely define who you are and the life you wish to live. Once you've decided on your values, you must incorporate them into your daily life via your decisions and actions.

Then boost your positivity. Begin spending time with positive individuals, absorbing their energy and utilizing them as motivation to pursue your ambitions. Finally, devote thirty days to honing your charm. The more attractive you seem, the more charming you are. This will boost your self-esteem as well as your confidence while dealing with others.

Follow Your Dreams: It's time to start making your ideas a reality once you've transformed yourself from the inside out.

Take some time to think about what you want to accomplish. Make it your goal to win the ideal lady, find the perfect career, or achieve some other life-changing goal.

Once you've decided on your mission, start defining objectives for how you're going to get there. Allow yourself thirty days to come up with a destination and a strong strategy to get there. Use the SMART technique to divide your overall objective into smaller, more attainable goals that can be properly monitored and tracked.

There is no dream too big for you now that you have grown the heart, intellect, and look of a real alpha guy. You may now begin to build the life you've always desired, the life of your dreams.

CHAPTER 6

GOALS IN LIFE

Are you looking for success? Goals are all about putting what you want to accomplish in the future into perspective and then going for it.

Have you ever wondered what makes one individual successful while another struggle? It's because they can establish objectives and then go for them with zeal.

Before we look at the advantages of goal setting and how to establish the appropriate objectives, let us first look at the many sorts of goals that may help you progress.

Goals of Various Types

Depending on what you aim to accomplish, goals may be classified in a variety of ways. You may create objectives for your company, education, personal life, or profession. Let's have a look at these sorts.

Educational Objectives

You must first study in order to progress and notice a difference in your life.

Learning is all about incorporating new knowledge into your system that you did not previously have. Education is more than simply a school; it includes vocational training, university, and even professional certificates.

These objectives will not stay constant as you go from one state to the next. The educational objectives you had ten years ago may not be the same aspirations you have now.

You must remember that education never ends. It is always lifelong, and you must attempt to broaden your mind in numerous ways.

The educational objectives that you set for yourself alter as you go, depending on the job route that you choose. When you have the capacity, you may choose to retrain your mind in a whole new field.

Relationship Objectives

While we may be complete in everything that we accomplish, we need others in our life to play that critical function in our lives - to feel loved and valued. Relationship objectives enable you to identify something that will improve your life while also benefiting others.

The better you become at attaining them, the more effect you'll have on the people around you, as well as your own pleasure.

You must make time for your family and friends in order to attain these objectives.

Physical Objectives

Our bodies, physical ability, and health all have a significant impact on the lives we lead and the things we can do. The objectives you set in this area are heavily influenced by your age and present condition of health.

If you are still young and healthy, the objectives you set will most likely be ones that will push you a little farther, such as a marathon.

If, on the other hand, you are in your forties and work at a desk all day, you may strive to keep your objectives within average limits for your age.

Personal Development Objectives

The only constant in life changes, and this applies to everyone - young and old. We may grow in a variety of ways depending on what we value the most.

It is entirely up to you whether you feel the need to extend yourself intellectually and physically by doing anything. You have the option of learning salsa, going to the gym, or mastering a new skill.

The necessity to set personal objectives is just that - you must examine what is going on in your life until you decide to make a change.

For personal growth to be effective, the desire to achieve must originate from the inside. You may extend your mind through reading, travelling across the globe, acquiring new talents, and working on yourself.

Financial Objectives

Money will affect how everything in your life works, including your relationships. This is why it is one of the most common topics to consider when it comes to planning and attaining objectives.

Making money is one of your motivations, no matter what job you are in.

If you have been unlucky enough to get indebted, you will resolve to keep a budget the next time you decide to spend money.

You must also modify your spending habits in order to accomplish things correctly.

Another common desire is to construct one's own home. Although it takes careful consideration, it will be beneficial if you opt to construct a home in the appropriate manner.

Retirement is another popular financial objective. You must give great consideration to when you will retire since you will not be receiving an income every month.

Career Objectives

We spend a large portion of our lives working, which is why it is essential to have a purpose in mind while doing so.

Education is linked to job aspirations since you cannot have a career without some level of education. So, you should strive to learn and then develop your skillset in order to open up new professional opportunities in your life.

Many individuals have a general concept of what they want out of their professions. You can want to achieve a certain honour, create your own company, or increase your earning capacity.

When you begin your career, you must construct a list of professional objectives that will serve as the foundation for a master plan that will guide your career progress. This is the first step toward a brighter future for you.

Spiritual Objectives

Spiritual objectives are another area that is linked to other aspects of your life for individuals who are religious. Personal growth and relationships are examples of this.

Whether you practice a particular religious' religion or not, developing your spiritual self- underpins practically everything you do.

You may set aside some time to undertake volunteer work or contribute extra money to those in need. Perhaps you'd want to serve as a missionary for a while before returning home. In any case, you must guarantee that the religious objectives you devise do not have an adverse effect on the people around you.

Goals Time magazine claims

Goals may either be long-term or short-term, depending on how much time you have available.

Long-term objectives are the plans you establish for the future – they are the ones that will normally take more than a year to complete.

Long-term objectives are often attained over time as a person progresses through the phases of life.

People develop long-term objectives because they anticipate what they want to achieve and where they want to be in five to twenty years.

Long-term objectives include the following:

- Obtain your master's degree.
- Purchase a larger home.
- Retire
- You have your own business.
- Run a marathon and finish it.

Short-term objectives, on the other hand, are those that you will reach quickly, generally in less than a year. They are often used as stepping stones to reach long-term objectives. Long-term objectives should be seen as a sequence of short-term goals that lead to your ultimate goal.

Examples of short-term objectives include:

- Participate in a gym membership
- Drop a couple of pounds
- Begin practising yoga.
- Get a high grade in the class.
- Get a job throughout the summer.
- Construct a gazebo.
- How to Set Appropriate Goals

Believe

Before you can start establishing goals, you must first believe in the process of goal setting. If you don't feel you can change your life to attain what you want, you should forget about making goals and try something else instead.

If you are unsure, take a glance at you; you will see that the beginning of anything is a notion. The notion is then converted into another form, such as a blueprint.

Visulize

After you have faith in something, the following stage is to picture what you want to happen.

If you need a business a year from now, you must first imagine the many adjustments that must occur before developing a plan—the clearer your vision, the greater your power to make it a reality.

Make a note of it

Writing down your dreams is an important element of achieving success. You become creative when you put down your ambitions. If you don't write these objectives down, you'll most likely forget about them. Make a point of writing down your objectives and keeping them somewhere you can see them every day.

Have a goal in mind.

The desire to reach the goal should motivate you to make adjustments in your life. You must understand why you should attain your objectives in the first place since this will lead you to your destination.

Knowing why you need something so badly can provide you with the drive to see it through to the end.

Make a commitment to the process.

This may seem to be a simple procedure, but it has serious ramifications if you ignore it. You must commit to the process of ensuring that you reach each objective. Understand why the objectives are essential to you, and then concentrate on ensuring that the result is correct.

When you commit to a goal, you must also concentrate on the outcomes.

If you get sidetracked, you will discover that you find yourself chasing objectives that have little bearing on your overall outcomes.

The good news is that you will be easily sidetracked if you do not practise often.

Make a plan.

If you want to reach your objectives, you must have a well-defined plan of action. Make a list of your objectives and break them down into stages so you can track your progress. When you have a plan of action, you will be able to revise it if anything goes wrong or if things aren't going as expected.

Take responsibility.

You must hold yourself responsible for what occurs if you are to persevere when things get difficult. Unless you have a coach who will do things for you, you must hold yourself responsible in all ways.

Try discussing your objectives with individuals close to you to help you remain accountable.

Conduct a review

Every time you examine the progress of your objectives, you must set aside a portion of the day to do so. When you evaluate your objectives on a regular basis, you will keep them fresh in your mind and turn them into practical tasks.

When you examine your objectives, you will remain aware of them and will not feel trapped if one does not work out since you will compensate for it elsewhere.

CHAPTER 7

DAILY HABITS AND EXERCISES TO BEAT PROCRASTINATION AND ACHIEVE YOUR GOALS

This chapter will discuss how to establish self-discipline to prevent procrastination and make your day more productive.

Let's get this party started.

1. Work on Your Goals Every Day

If you want to achieve what you tell others you want to do, you must work on it. If you wait until the last minute to work on your objectives, you will struggle to get started since you will not have built up a significant amount of momentum.

2. Make a Workable Schedule

It's easy to give up and declare, "There aren't enough hours in the day!" But it is just not the case. Sure, you have a lot to do in life, and it may seem that there aren't enough hours in the day to get everything done, but you can simply manage your calendar to create space for what you want to get done.

3. Make Time for Social Activities

Many individuals are fantastic at establishing plans to hang out with friends, but they are horrible at following through on such commitments. If you want to be a self-disciplined, productive human being, you must arrange socialising so that you may do all of the enjoyable things you want to do. And, no, this does not imply that your social life takes precedence over other elements of your life.

4. Make Sure You're Sleeping

Diet, exercise, and work hours are vital, but they're useless if you're not getting enough sleep. If you are weary most of the time, you will not be as productive at work or in your personal life. Sleep 7-8 hours every night to feel rejuvenated throughout the day, and stay up late if you need to get everything done during the day.

5. Establish Accountability Systems

Most individuals fail to achieve their objectives simply because they are not responsible.

If you're attempting to persuade yourself to do anything, tell someone else that you'll hold yourself responsible for it and let them know what you've agreed to do. This accountability system works better than the "I'll do it on my own" way because it provides someone with the capacity to hold you responsible if things go wrong—and it provides you with a support network if things go well and you want to rejoice.

6. Hire a Coach/Mentor

If you're attempting to accomplish something you've never done before, it can be a good idea to hire a coach or mentor so you can obtain advice from someone who's been there. You don't have to take their advice, but it's helpful to have someone provide feedback and support while striving toward your objectives.

7. Create Goal-Achieving Procedures

If you want to achieve long-term objectives, you'll need some systems in place to help you remain on track.

Make a plan and a strategy for achieving your objectives. This will assist you in keeping your eye on the prize while being organised with all of the information required to attain your objective.

8. Focus on Smaller Portions of the Bigger Picture

If something seems to be too enormous to do, break it down into smaller parts so you can feel like you're making progress. If you can build tiny systems and processes for each element of your goal, you'll be able to check off each item as you go and feel more inspired to keep working toward your overall objective.

9. Set a realistic goal for yourself and commit to it

If you want to achieve a certain objective, it must be within your degree of expertise. There's no use in working towards a goal if you're not driven to reach it. If you haven't previously accomplished your objective, don't set yourself up for failure by attempting anything excessively ambitious.

If you can do things to help you achieve your objective, make sure you do them so that the chances are in your favour.

10. Commit to the Goal in Advance

If you're going to commit to a particular goal, do so well before the commitment date so you have time to prepare. If you wait until your commitment date, you are less likely to complete the task than if you commit ahead of time.

11. Remind yourself of your goals regularly

Once you've chosen a goal for yourself, you must stick to it throughout the year. Some individuals make the mistake of establishing a goal and then ignoring it until the following year. You must maintain concentration on your objectives to achieve them.

12. Be Involved in Your Goal and the Process of Reaching It

The key to reaching a goal is not just working towards it but also being involved in the process of working towards it. You can't expect to succeed unless you actively strive toward your objective.

Strive to reach your objectives, but keep in mind that you must work to make your ambitions a reality. There is no way to avoid personal development, so simply do the work and enjoy the process of achieving whatever you set out to achieve.

13. Make Slow, But Continuous Progress

If you want to reach a huge goal, you'll need to make consistent progress toward that objective. If you initially leap in and make a lot of progress, you're likely to fade as the objective becomes more difficult.

14. Find a Community to Help You Achieve Your Goals

Ideally, you'll surround yourself with individuals who share your interests and who will support you as you work toward your objective. Participating in a community of like-minded individuals may help generate responsibility for your objectives and keep you on track.

CHAPTER 8

STRATEGIES TO BECOME

MOTIVATED

Strategy 1

Maintaining Spiritual Motivation

As a Christian, I find that focusing on the fact that I think God has a plan for my life (and I believe He does for yours) makes it much simpler for me to look past difficult times to a different sort of future.

You may not share my Christian views, but spiritual issues may drive you. Everyone, I believe, gets a sense of serenity when they are linked to the idea that there is something larger than us that we may not be able to see or touch.

Whatever it is for you, engaging with it daily may help to focus your thoughts, behaviours, and life in general.

My personal experience has taught me to set aside time each day (usually first thing in the morning) to read my bible, complete a bible study, and spend time in prayer and worship.

If you are not at ease with the notion of prayer but like the idea of quieting your thoughts, you may want to consider the method using meditation, which may have a similar impact.

Strategy 2

Establishing a Special Journal

The most significant benefit of maintaining a diary is that it helps you keep a full record of what is going on in your life as you go about your everyday activities. You'll keep a notebook to document what occurs as you work toward your objectives. This will assist you in remaining motivated throughout the day.

How Should You Use Your Journal?

1. When you accomplish an item on your to-do list that moves you closer to your goal, write a "congratulations" note to yourself and note how nice it felt to finish the item.
2. If you cannot complete a task or remain motivated at times, write it down in your diary. Write down why you're down and what occurred that day to make you lose your motivating spirit.

3. Always have your diary with you.

Now, the next time you're feeling down and unmotivated to work on your objectives, open your diary and look for a day when you had a terrible day and read what you did to cheer yourself up. Look for any occurrences that have repeatedly undermined your motivation.

For example, after reading your diary, you may realize that whenever you have a lengthy meeting at work, you feel angry and avoid focusing on your objectives. Reading your list of items that inspire you can help you psychologically prepare for your next planned meeting. Alternatively, listen to your tape where you discussed your hopes and objectives and let that motivate you.

Your attitude going into the meeting will carry you through it and prevent you from having a "motivational breakdown" later on.

Strategy 3

Make a Vision Board

Vision boards are an excellent method to stay inspired in your life by utilizing pictures that remind you of your goals and aspirations. Here are a few basic methods to make a vision board keep yourself inspired.

Tools for Creating a Basic Vision Board

1. Purchase a poster board or corkboard from a pharmacy or office supply shop.
2. Colored marker set
3. Scissors
4. Pushpins for the corkboard/poster board adhesive
5. Photographs of family and acquaintances.
6. Magazines contain pictures of what you desire in your life. For example, photos of distant locations you'd want to visit, residences, vehicles, and so on...

Place your poster board, pictures, and magazine images on your poster board or corkboard. You may be as creative as you want. As an example, put your name underneath the automobile of your dreams or the date you want to visit Spain. Put images of your children and spouse, as well as other photos that inspire you every day, in a prominent location where you can see them.

Place your vision board somewhere you will see it regularly.

Seeing your ambitions portrayed graphically can drive you to keep working on your ideas every day.

Using Your Computer Tools to Create a Vision Board

1. A computer, a Mac, or a tablet
2. Photographs and images

Make a vision board on your PC. You do not need any specialized software. You may make your board using easy picture software already on your computer. Arrange your photographs as you would on a poster board, adding motivating phrases for yourself and anything else you need to keep encouraged.

You may also want to check out Pinterest, a pretty unique social network that allows you to easily build online visual boards of the things that inspire you the most.

Strategy 4

The Sound of Music!

When you're having a poor day and don't feel motivated about anything, listening to music that makes you feel good about yourself may be a strong component that gets you straight back on track with your positive inspiration.

Music Selection

Because everyone's musical tastes vary, only you can choose what kind of music uplifts your soul. Whatever you choose, try to listen to music with positive lyrics that encourage you to dream big and see the possibilities in life.

There are performers from every genre of music who have created great-sounding uplifting music, and there are just too many to name here.

How to Find Uplifting Music in Any Genre

You can find music to buy and download to your MP3 player, computer, or smartphone by searching on iTunes, Amazon, and hundreds of other websites. Make a motivational album with music from as many different artists and genres as you desire. Then, after you've found a music mix you like, listen to it anytime you're feeling uninspired. Make a point of getting back to work on your plan. You may even listen while working on your game plan to gain an additional injection of inspiration.

- Gospel Music Categories
- Rock 'n' Roll Christian
- Classical Pop Rock
- R&B
- Adult Latino Contemporary

Another genre with a lot of motivating music is movie soundtracks. Beautiful music played by some of the world's top orchestras may be found on select soundtracks.

Support Groups are a fifth strategy.

These days, support groups can be found almost everywhere. Some organizations meet regularly, even once a week. Getting together with like-minded people to help you remain inspired is a terrific approach to keep your aspirations and objectives alive.

Where to Look for Support Groups

1. Investigate your church or other places of worship.
2. Local community centers and non-profit groups
3. If you're planning to establish your own company, the Small Business Administration may provide information on local clubs that might help you remain focused.
4. Check with your local library since they may have information about clubs in your area.
5. Local community colleges are a great location to get help.
6. Look online for local support groups as well as online chat groups, teleconferences, and web conferences.

Begin Your Own

You may create your own support group if you have the time and inclination. You may also think about forming a mastermind group. A mastermind group is a collection of like-minded people working toward the same objectives. Mastermind groups are often focused on creating your own company, attaining objectives, or having a good mentality.

Strategy 6

Motivational Sermons

I like listening to sermons that inspire, encourage, make me laugh, and nourish my soul! Some of the most inspiring sermons I've ever heard have come from Joel Osteen, TD Jakes, and others. If you are unable to view sermons when they show on television because of time constraints, you can usually access free replays on their websites, and most also provide podcasts that you may download and listen to at any time.

If your faith is waning, seeing an inspirational sermon from your favorite pastor might be the spiritual shot in the arm you need to concentrate.

Where Can I Find Motivational Sermons?

1. You may buy sermons straight from your favorite pastors' websites or from big retailers such as Amazon.
2. Conduct an internet search using Google or Bing.
3. If you have a DVR, you can record sermons and view them later when it is more convenient for you.
4. If Christian sermons aren't your style, you may discover a plethora of different motivating speeches and presentations utilising the same sorts of materials online.

Strategy 7

Rewards

Another strategy to keep yourself motivated is to reward yourself as you go through your objectives. This method works particularly effectively if your objectives take a long time to achieve.

Create a reward system to applaud yourself when you achieve a goal, as well as when you don't. The idea is to reward yourself for achieving a goal while also keeping you motivated when you fall short on occasion. You aren't encouraging failure; instead, you are awarding yourself for adhering to your plan and giving it your best.

Rewards

You may choose the kind of prizes you want to give yourself, but here are a few suggestions.

1. A day at the spa
2. Your favorite place for dinner
3. Buy yourself new clothing.
4. A day excursion to see vineyards, orchards, or other comparable locations
5. A book from a favorite author
6. Fragrance or cologne
7. Host a barbecue with your buddies.
8. Have a makeover
9. Acquire a new skill
10. Attend a movie or a play.

I'm sure you can think of a number of various ways to reward yourself. Just make sure you do it on a regular basis. Even if you are the one rewarding yourself, the prospect of receiving a reward will keep you motivated. If you tell yourself that you will reward yourself with a vacation to a day spa if you successfully keep to your plan every day for a week, you will be more driven to reach that objective.

Strategy 8

Set smaller objectives. First

Having too many objectives may be daunting at times, and attempting to keep up with them all might make you want to give up. Setting modest objectives initially allows you to remain motivated without feeling obligated to do everything at once.

How Do You Set Smaller Objectives?

Larger objectives may take longer to achieve, and you may get disheartened if it takes too long. Setting minor objectives that lead to your final goal can increase your chances of success along the road, which will help you remain motivated.

1. Determine a key objective that you want to achieve.
2. Determine the minor objectives that must be met in order to achieve the larger goal. For example, if you're frightened of heights and want to overcome your anxiety by skydiving

for the first time, you may start by doing a few jumps in a simulated skydiving facility. This will motivate you to remain focused on your ultimate objective no matter how long you have to wait till you make the big leap.

If you follow these procedures for each of your objectives, you will not be sidetracked while working toward your larger goals.

Strategy 9

Inform Others of Your Goals/Plans

If you want to remain inspired in a large manner, assemble all of your friends and family and tell them what your main objective is and how you intend to attain it. Then set aside time in the future to show them how far you've come.

If you pick this technique, you will be tremendously driven to follow through on what you promised your family and friends. It puts extra pressure on you to follow through on your objectives, but it also keeps you tremendously motivated. The last thing you want to do is inform your family and friends that you've given up!

How to Communicate Your Goals to Others?

Host a casual get-together with your closest friends and family.

Make it joyful and enjoyable.

Select an acceptable time to inform everyone about your objectives, aspirations, and goals, as well as when you want to attain them.

It will be up to you to keep on track and focused so that you can report your accomplishments afterwards. Accountability may be a powerful motivator for certain individuals.

Strategy 10

Put some of the fun aside for later.

When working on your objectives, try not to plan the most enjoyable activities all at once. Distribute some of the enjoyment throughout the procedure. The enjoyment might come from the many milestones and/or prizes that you offer yourself as you work toward your goal.

Setting up a reward plan first, then looking at your calendar and seeing where you can fit in rewards, is the greatest approach to spread out your enjoyment.

When you find yourself not crossing off your objectives as quickly as you would like, take a break and use one of your enjoyable rewards to help yourself feel better and ready yourself to come back to your plan and keep moving ahead.

CHAPTER 9

TIPS AND TRICKS TO GET

THINGS DONE IN LESS TIME

Perfectionism is sought for by one sort of procrastinator.

They put off starting the job until the last minute. Even when they are just getting started on the project, they whine about not having enough time to finish it. When they postpone a task, these procrastinators usually make fantastic excuses.

You may be busy and have a lot to accomplish, but overworking is not the way to become a productive person or prevent procrastination. When individuals fail to meet deadlines, they attempt to blame the deadline, yet it is evident that it has nothing to do with their failure. It is all their fault since they procrastinated. However, most individuals seldom accept it.

You will not be able to work with a comfortable mentality if you wait until the deadline. You will not provide your best effort if you are not calm. Focus on your objectives if you don't want procrastination to come your way. Make sure to separate your objectives in a manner that allows you to attain them. Also, keep in mind that if you do not comprehend the importance of your objective, you will not hesitate to postpone it.

To attain your objectives, you must first recognize their worth. People may delay because they lack self-confidence and believe they will not complete the allotted activity. However, just thinking about it causes them to postpone their job and strain. Then they begin to question if they will accomplish the assignment on time.

I won't advise you should become a productive person immediately after reading this book (since it is just impossible), but you should strive to make small changes at a time. Procrastination may be conquered if you are proactive.

Accept the fact that you dislike working under extreme pressure.

Lawyers, ER surgeons, and politicians, for example, like working under duress. That's fantastic if you can accomplish any of these things! You're misguided if you believe you're exceptional at working under pressure. The underlying cause for your overwork is that you have postponed the work, and you now need to task hard if you want to finish the project.

Furthermore, you do not want to underperform, which is why you believe that you work better under pressure. The only choice you have is to not put off doing an assignment until the final minute.

Make use of the Pomodoro Technique.

You may manage your job by using this time management strategy. You will work for 25 minutes and then rest for five minutes. You may use this strategy anytime you have a job that has been postponed or when you are allocated a large assignment. Instead of thinking, "I'd have to spend my whole life to complete this assignment," you might say, "I'll use the Pomodoro Technique."

It will help you keep concentrated if you know you just have to focus on a segment for 25 minutes, and then you may take a five-minute break. This is one of the most effective strategies for getting things done.

Do Your Best.

For example, you may be required to create an eBook. The book must then be divided into chapters. You will feel more in control if you have split the chapters. Furthermore, some chapters may be simple and others that are tougher. However, due to the degree of complexity, not everyone can work. As a result, simply write if you want to accomplish the first. Don't assume you have to accomplish the difficult ones first and then the easier ones. It doesn't work like that. You must do all in your power!

Nominate Someone

You must designate someone to follow up with you if you fail to fulfil the deadlines. It might be your parents or friends, but you must answer them. You might ask them why you haven't fulfilled a certain goal you set for yourself. But that person must be firm and consistent with you!

Don't Try to Multitask

You may have been misled into believing that multitasking is advantageous. But believe me, it is not! When you multitask, you tend to lose focus on your duties. Of course, some individuals can multitask, but you should avoid doing so if you are not one of them. You will jeopardise the quality of all your work by multitasking, which will lead to more problems. Furthermore, it may cause you to delay your task. Instead of multitasking, you may focus on one job at a time and perform your best for that activity.

Exercise

If you believe that exercising when you have work to complete is a kind of procrastination, you are mistaken! It's simple to get sidetracked when you don't have enough drive to achieve anything.

It's simple to avoid doing it. As a result, if you are not mood to work, you will postpone.

Instead of delaying, consider concentrating on some exercise.

The activity will increase your endorphin levels and make you happy. You may discover numerous workouts online, so look for several and save them. Exercise might help you feel better when you're feeling down or unproductive!

When you procrastinate, be aware that you are responsible.

Even though we all delay, we tend to feel bad about it when we confront the repercussions. There may have been moments when you lost out on several fantastic opportunities due to your procrastination. And there may be days when you labour all night to make a deadline. There may be occasions when you must abandon friends to complete the assignment before the customer becomes enraged. Consider all of these scenarios and embrace the truth that you are a procrastinator. Once you accept this, you will gradually conquer the problem. Acceptance is also the most effective method to get things done.

Consider the End Result

What will happen if you put this work off? What may be the worst outcome of postponing this project? Fear is associated with procrastination.

You may utilise this fear to your advantage when it comes to procrastinating. How? It is rather straightforward. You just need to consider the consequences of postponing a project. Consider your boss's furious expression or a colleague's disappointed expression. Consider the repercussions of postponing the project. And when you do, you will naturally be afraid of the mess you will make. As a result, you will attempt not to postpone the task. The concept of using fear to your advantage will assist you in avoiding procrastination.

Take Care of Yourself

Small incentives may not always fulfil your need for recognition. Also, if you are better than before at avoiding procrastination, you should reward yourself with something significant. After you finish the job, you must determine what you want to do. And the burning desire to have fun will improve your job and make you more productive.

Simply Do It

"Just do it," as the popular motto goes, because you have to do it!

It's your project and your duty. You have accepted responsibility for doing it. Therefore, you cannot evade or find excuses not to do it! One of the most prevalent reasons for procrastination is a lack of motivation to accomplish a job. Why don't you want to finish the task? The answer is irrelevant since if you have accepted the work, you are accountable for doing it, so just do it! You must comprehend the reality that you have accepted labor. As a result, you must do it. Allow it to sink in.

If it does, you may find yourself not waiting until the last possible moment to accomplish a job.

That being said, getting things done depends entirely on how you think! Your thinking is the driving force behind getting things done. Consider. Act. And triumph!

CHAPTER 10

HABITS YOU SHOULD

DEVELOP TO BECOME AN ALPHA MALE

In this chapter, you'll discover additional alpha male behaviors that you may adopt to become one.

Overcome Your Fears

To become an alpha guy, you must learn to enjoy life to the utmost.

Alpha guys have acquired the art of overcoming their apprehension about the unknown.

They've learnt to accept pain to pursue something they're enthusiastic about. They are aware that there may be difficulties in achieving their objectives, yet they are nevertheless prepared to take the risk.

Make a list of the things in life that you are terrified of. Consider every situation in which fear prevents you from enjoying your life to the fullest.

You've undoubtedly gained weight and are concerned that others will mock you if you go gym. Or maybe you're locked in a toxic relationship and are frightened that if you leave, you'll never find another woman to love again.

Whatever it is, make a note of it. When you're finished, ask yourself, "What might be the worst thing that could happen?"

What is the nicest thing that might happen?

How long would it take for me to get back on my feet if I failed?

You'd be astonished to learn that when you consider what you're terrified of, the worst-case scenarios may not be as horrible as you anticipated.

Get out of your comfort zone and start living!

Don't Let Anyone Tell You Which Way to Go.

Alpha guys have a strong vision and goal in mind. They are clear about what they want to accomplish with their life. This is how they inspire others.

They know what they want, and they don't allow others to tell them where they should go to get it. Make a plan, then take action. You must fulfil your destiny.

Strive for Consistent Progress

The main competition for alpha guys is themselves. They'll never be found wallowing in self-pity because others are more successful than him. They don't compare themselves to others.

They may not have achieved success yet, but they know that modest victories will ultimately lead them to their ultimate objective.

So don't be concerned if your life isn't as nice as your friends'. Life success does not happen in an instant. It's a process that you must go through in order to enjoy your achievement more.

Don't Fight Just for the Purpose of It.

Instead of beginning a fight, alpha guys believe in taking action and learning. They would not spend their time debating their ideas, religion, philosophy, and politics on the internet or among their friends. Instead, they are devoted to doing the things they know will help them develop.

This is not to say that you should avoid intellectual conversations and arguments. The trick is to reach an agreement to disagree.

Do what is right because it is the right thing to do.

Alpha guys are kind and have a strong desire to help others. But they are not doing this to gain popularity; rather, they are doing it because they are decent people.

- They provide assistance to others without expecting anything in return.
- They really care about people and have empathy for them.
- They feel that the only thing that counts is how you affect other people.

Every day when you wake up, ask yourself, "What good can I do today?"

Always Speak the Truth.

When alpha men have a strong conviction in anything, they will not hesitate to defend that opinion.

The alpha guy expresses himself, yet with consideration for others.

They will not give up on whatever they believe in. While he respects other people's viewpoints, he will not be influenced by them.

Speak your thoughts, even if it means upsetting others. Be self-assured enough to take a stance.

Improve Your Self-Sufficiency

An alpha male is a man in his own right. He encourages self-sufficiency. He understands he has the authority to make his own decisions since they know it is the best option.

However, being self-sufficient does not exclude you from seeking assistance from friends or neighbours. There will be times when you must accept that you need assistance.

Create a Strong Body

You don't need six-pack abs or 20-inch biceps to be an alpha dude. However, in order to have a strong physique, you must be both physically and mentally healthy. You owe it to yourself and others to look after your own well-being.

You can't fully enjoy life if your body isn't robust and healthy.

You Should Be Able to Defend Yourself

To be able to protect oneself, you must be physically healthy, which links back to the previous habit. Every guy should learn to fight at some time in his life. However, simple self-defence tactics might suffice.

Take good care of yourself.

Self-care is essential, particularly for dominant males. Your health and well-being should be your primary priority.

Begin by doing one act of self-care every day. You may want to try meditation. Alternatively, you may attempt something you like doing, such as a pastime, one day. Visit a sauna or get a massage.

So, don't disregard your health.

Follow Your Values

You should follow your code. Define and live by your ideals.

Live your life with honesty.

Most individuals experience sadness and anxiety as a result of living a life that is not in accordance with their ideals.

Don't claim that your family is vital while spending more time working.

Spend time with your family if you want to have a good family life.

Do you want to be happy? Then everything you do, everything you say, and everything you think should be in sync.

Determine what is essential to you. If it's family, go ahead and do it. If it's a financial success, go for it. If you want to embark on an adventure on your own, go for it. If you pursue these activities, you will not lose your status as an alpha guy.

Keep Your Promises

Because your word is your honour, you must maintain it. If you say you'll do something, make it happen. If you say you're not going to do it, then don't. That's a simple idea to understand.

Keeping your word builds trust among those who follow you. Your reputation would benefit as well. Most importantly, you learn to believe in yourself.

Your words are powerful, so choose them carefully.

Failure to keep your promise will make it easy for you to lose faith. Whatever you say will have no effect because no one will trust you if you continue to break your promises.

You're human, and you get tired, so don't overextend yourself.

Make commitments that you are certain you will be able to keep. If you are doubtful, do not make a commitment. It is preferable to say "no" early rather than breach your word later because you did not have the luxury of time.

In today's environment, it's difficult to find a guy that keeps his promise regardless of the circumstances.

Don't let yourself become one of those guys.

Master the Art of Attraction, Charm, and Seduction

You should be able to attract particular sorts of individuals who can assist you in reaching your objectives. Similarly, if starting a family is one of your key ambitions, you should look for a lady with whom you can share your life.

Improving your confidence can help you become more charismatic.

Make Your Life Difficult, and Enjoy Sweet Victory Later

You must realise that alpha men do not want a simple existence; their primary purpose is to progress, not to live in luxury and comfort.

They understand that the difficulties and hardships they will face will make them stronger. These will help children develop character and educate them to be resilient. Make the unpleasant your new comfort.

Be Willing to Die for a Cause in Which You Believe In

Alpha guys are prepared to die for something or anyone they love.

They will die fighting for their family, their honour, their principles, and so on.

It takes a lot of effort to become the alpha guy. It is a journey that does not occur overnight.

You may have to endure discomfort and trials, as well as suffering, but it will all be worthwhile in the end.

CHAPTER 11

TROUBLESHOOTING:

IF SELF-DISCIPLINE ISN'T WORKING FOR

YOU

The Difficulty of Striking a Balance Between Accountability and Strictness

This book's material is based on human psychology, insights from classic research studies, and near-universal facts about how people think and behave. As a result, the tips and methods will 'work' for most individuals if they put in enough effort.

However, the transition from a careless lifestyle with bad mental habits to a disciplined life will not be easy! As a result, the last portion of this book is devoted to troubleshooting. If you've done all you can to take what's stated herein and still can't seem to go on in your life, you'll find some helpful tips below. You must establish a balance between consistency and reasonable expectations; demand the best from yourself while also realizing that self-discipline does not emerge overnight.

The first issue is a lack of patience.

If you've just been working on self-discipline for a few days or even weeks and you're already upset, your main issue is a lack of patience.

Allow yourself some time. You may have spent months or years instilling in yourself some extremely undesirable behaviors and negative thought patterns.

So, doesn't it make sense that learning to live in a new and better manner would take time? Take it one week at a time, or perhaps one day at a time.

Remember that self-disciplined individual considers their mentality a lifetime endeavor, so you should constantly be on the lookout for signals that you are reverting to detrimental thought patterns. While it is a waste of time to criticize yourself for lack of development, keep in mind that self-improvement never really has an ending! Get in the habit of working on yourself daily.

Problem Number Two: Changing the Alignment of Goals and Values

If you have worked hard to develop appropriate objectives but find yourself unable to accomplish them, reconsider if they correspond with your beliefs. Setting 'must-and should-based do's on value systems other than your own will make it difficult to retain momentum when things become tough. And, since this is real life, things will become difficult at some time. When this occurs, the objectives based on the shakiest assumptions or the worst values will be the first to suffer.

Problem Three: Failure to Use External Accountability

Although this book is about self-discipline, you would be remiss if you ignored the role that other people may play in assisting you in living a productive and successful life. While you always must choose your life's direction and purpose, self-aware and self-disciplined individuals understand that others may be a great resource in assisting them in staying on track.

Seek out others who are trying similar self-improvement.

Attend local events or join online forums where you may meet individuals passionate about personal growth and are prepared to put in every ounce of effort to be the greatest version of themselves. Find individuals with whom you can share your goals, struggles, and triumphs. To take it a step further, you may create a contract with one or more individuals to keep each other responsible. Some cities, for example, have 'breakfast clubs,' which are gatherings in which everyone in attendance takes turns discussing the progress they are making with their initiatives and aspirations. Each individual then seeks responsibility and criticism from others.

While it may seem to be fully collaborative on the surface, each participant displays a great level of self-discipline by regularly coming in the first place! Remember, no one is going to yank you off the couch and force you to meet or chat with your accountability partner (s). Choosing the appropriate individuals to assist push you to new heights is an important part of accepting responsibility for your own life.

Fourth, there is a lack of creativity.

At times, there may seem to be no apparent cause for your lack of self-discipline. Assume you're taking good care of your body, focusing on your attitude, and creating appropriate objectives for yourself. Life is going well for you, yet you have an underlying feeling of restlessness and discontent. What may be the source of the problem?

One option is that you don't include enough imagination in your daily life. Most people identify the term "creativity" with the visual arts – drawing, painting, and so on – but anybody who actively strives to produce new ideas and ways of life is creative. This idea of going on a new journey and creating something unique may give you a great burst of energy, increasing your self-discipline.

Examine your day-to-day activities. Do you believe you have the ability to express yourself creatively? Do you have at least one passion or leisure that enables you to play, experiment with other concepts and ideas, or at the very least consider living in new ways? If not, it may be time to look for one. Your chosen creative activity does not have to be directly tied to your objectives, but the happiness and energy it brings will permeate other parts of your life. Furthermore, completing a creative task — whether it is a new cuisine, a short novel, or redesigning your living space – will provide you with a feeling of accomplishment, which will increase your self-esteem. As a result, you are more inclined to pursue your most treasured objectives with fresh zeal.

Problem Number Five: Inadequate Underlying Self-Esteem

Some of us desire to improve our lives, yet we are repeatedly hindered by the same old foe — ourselves. If you've been establishing goals and making changes in your life to achieve them but haven't seen any progress after a few months, despite your best efforts, it may be time to dig a bit further into the causes of your self-sabotage. It might be tough to realise that the only thing standing in your way of a better life is yourself, yet the most painful truths are often the ones we most need to hear.

Aside from sloth, the most typical reason for self-sabotage is a deep-seated belief that you do not deserve the lifestyle you want.

Sure, it's important to establish objectives and adopt thinking methods that will help you achieve them. Still, if you don't believe deep down that you are deserving of the type of life you desire, you'll discover that all your goals stay elusive, and life never seems fully satisfactory.

What's the answer? If you feel you have a problem with this and have struggled for a long time, it may be time to seek professional treatment. This is nothing to be embarrassed about; some of the most successful and motivated individuals have had therapists, and life coaches assist them in understanding why they have been locked in such self-destructive behaviors. Obtaining this kind of assistance is not a sign of weakness but rather of self-awareness and determination to achieve your objectives. These are two attributes that are required for self-discipline.

You may discover a qualified therapist or life coach by seeking referrals from trustworthy friends and/or medical experts. If feasible, request to talk with some of their prior clientele or, at the very least, read testimonials. Most therapists and coaches provide free introductory sessions or consultations, so don't be hesitant to test out two or three before selecting the ideal one for you. According to research, the essential aspect is the result of any therapy or coaching is the connection or "fit" between practitioner and client. Thus it is well worth waiting until you find someone with whom you can work effectively.

CHAPTER 12

THE IMPORTANCE OF A HEALTHY LIFESTYLE AND NUTRITION

The food we eat is one of the most important distinctions in our life. Many Americans do not consume a healthy diet, and a sizable proportion of the population is fat. Many doctors believe that stress and the influx of people suffering from depression result from a vitamin deficiency. The stress that many of us are feeling today may result from not eating a balanced diet.

We all know that proper nutrition is essential for a healthy body, but what about a healthy mind? We hear about the importance of a healthy diet for both physical and mental health.

Certain foods are natural mood boosters. These are as follows:

- **Milk and dairy products:** Dairy is often rich in protein and may improve bodily response to stress. You may consume dairy in the form of milk or cheese and anticipate fewer bodily troubles as a result of stress and have a better mood.
- **Fish:** High-fat fish, such as salmon, are beneficial to both the body and the mind. We all know that fish is considered brain food, but fish rich in Omega-3 fats is a natural approach to cope with depression. According to several research, people who suffer from stress-related depression have low amounts of Omega-3 fats in their blood.
- **Turkey** is another dish that boosts serotonin levels. Turkey contains tryptophan, an amino acid that helps you relax.

Remember how exhausted you were after eating Thanksgiving dinner last year? That came from tryptophan, a natural sedative.

- **Nuts from Brazil** One of them is selenium, also a mood booster. However, too much of these nuts might be hazardous to your system, so take them in moderation.

- **Complex carbs** also include tryptophan, and although we have been advised to avoid carbohydrates in recent years, we want complex carbs rather than simple carbs.

If you aren't receiving enough of these items in your daily diet, consider taking a multivitamin or supplement. If you are stressed, you may be deficient in vitamin B and Omega-3 fatty acids.

Eating a proper diet plan will not harm you and may end up removing a lot of your tension.

Exercise is also essential for stress reduction. When you sense tension building up, the greatest thing you can do to combat it is exercise. Doing something physical may often help you solve your problem.

Cardio activities are the most effective way to relieve stress. These get your heart rate up and naturally enhance serotonin levels in your brain, putting you in a much better mood. Stress may be highly taxing on your physical being, but exercise can help you right the wrong and get your body back in shape. Exercise also boosts the immune system, which helps the body deal with stress.

Get yourself into a workout routine. Exercise in the morning or after work, completing cardiovascular activities that will improve both your body and mind, as well as help you manage stress. At night, you may do yoga or stretching activities that will help you tone your body while also calming you.

Do you not want to exercise? Perform physical activity. Cleaning up the kitchen floor cannot just relieve your tension. It will also thoroughly clean the floor. Physical activity, such as cleaning, is one of the most effective stress relievers available. It works far better than any tablet, it's free, and when you're through, you'll have a wonderfully clean house.

CONCLUSION

Being aware of how your mind operates is the first step toward self-discipline. Recognize that your conscience and impulse control are two separate voices in your brain. The difficulty is knowing when to listen to and being self-aware of your thoughts throughout the day. Self-control will become simpler if you can make it a habit. Your brain will have greater influence over you since it knows what is best for you (self-control) better than any external force (impulse). This is similar to how two individuals might be equally powerful, but one will have more self-control.

Self-discipline is a talent that can be learned with practice by anybody. It's not something you either have or don't have. A lack of self-control is not a weakness, and it is surely not a deficiency in one's character. Self-discipline is the process of exceeding the constraints of your primitive brain and establishing control over your life to attain better levels of success than others. It will become simpler to handle if you make it a habit. Be mindful of your willpower's strength. If you're out of shape, don't give up on yourself and create goals you know you'll break since you'll simply give up again.

Begin slowly and be honest with yourself. Consider which form of incentive is most successful for you. When you fulfil a short-term objective, reward yourself. Don't be too hard or too soft on yourself.

Don't penalise yourself if you don't accomplish what you set to achieve.

Remember, self-discipline is an action-based skill that must be intentionally exercised! Your mind can positively lead and affect your actions.

Thank you for taking the time to read this, and best of luck!